MW00614558

CINCINNATI & SOUP

Recipes from the Queen City and Great Soup

BY CHERI BRINKMAN

ISBN-10: 0-615-36001-7
ISBN-13: 978-0-6153-6001-0

ALL RIGHTS RESERVED

CINCINNATI AND SOUP ©2010

First Edition 2010
THIRD PRINTING 2012

Mac Guffin Productions
cincinnatiandsoup@yahoo.com
www.VintageCincinnati.Etsy.com

Cover & Design:
Erin Beckloff :: iNkY WiNKe
inkywinky.etsy.com

Postcard (Cover Art):
Skyline from Ohio River, Cincinnati,Ohio
Kraemer Art. Co. Cincinnati, Ohio circa 1940

The brand-names mentioned in this book are trademarks
or registered trademarks of their respective companies.

To Ed Brinkman, Allison Brinkman
and all of those who have reveled
in my cooking over the years.

To my family and friends
without whose encouragement
this would not have happened.

Blessings to all!

This is a collection of recipes from aging yellow cards, notes and memories. This began as a collection of special "homemade soups" but as time went on there has seemed to be a great interest in some of the great recipes of the Cincinnati area to be preserved.

Some of these recipes are nostalgic in nature. Some are credited to local television programs where they were copied down from or classic products which "everyone from Cincinnati" knows or has heard of. This collection is especially too for those friends and relatives who have "moved away" and long for a familiar taste of home.

So let's start cooking! and Bon Appetit!!!

Cheri Brinkman
2010

Cincinnati Favorites

Modern "Quick" Goetta!   9
Homemade Ohio Chili   11
Recipes Using Chili   12-13
Cincinnati Style Chili   14-15
Mock Turtle Soup   17
The Cincinnati Slider   18-19
Cincinnati Hamburger Pizza   21
BBQ Chicken Pizza   23
Pogue's French Salad Dressing   25
Hotel Sinton's Spring Pea Salad   27
Deli-Style Potato Pancakes   29
Apple Tart Francais   31
Shillito's® 7 Hills Bar-B-Q Sandwich   33

TV Treats from the 1950-60's

UNCLE AL'S

The Black Cow/ The Pink Cow   35

RUTH LYONS

Cranberry-Cherry Gelatin Salad   38
Coffee Cake   39

GOETTA!

The original recipe for goetta calls for going by the stock yards for a large bag of pork bones, then cooking them for about 8 to 10 hours in a stock pot for the main meat substance of the dish. As most of us do NOT live near the stockyards now days and most of the stock yards would not give us a bag of pork bones, we need to bow to modern ways. No more 10 hour boiling! We now have a lower fat and quick recipe for this favorite local dish.

Ways to Serve Goetta:

1. Fry up in a pan and serve on toast with topped with an egg "over easy."

2. Serve as a "side" at breakfast with eggs and toast. May be topped with maple syrup.

3. Can be served in a number of recipes including as a pizza topping or in a burrito.

Burrito: Using a flour tortilla, spread cream cheese over tortilla, add fried goetta in crumble size pieces. Top with chopped lettuce, tomatoes and cheese. Salsa may be added if you choose.

MODERN "QUICK" GOETTA!

1 roll sage sausage
1 cup pinhead or steel cut oats
1 cup onions or 3 teasp dehydrated onions
½ teasp salt
1 teasp dried red pepper flakes
1 teasp ground black pepper.
water

DIRECTIONS:
In a large pot put the 3 cups of water. Break the sausage into small bits and add to the water along with the onions. Cook for about 10 min over a medium heat.

IN MICROWAVE:
Mix 2 cups of water with 1 cup of oatmeal and ½ teasp salt. Microwave 3 min. Then stir. Do this 3 times (9-12 min. total)

Drain the sausage and onion (this removes a lot of the grease and fat from the goetta). Add the oatmeal mixture to the pan. Add the peppers. Mix. Put in loaf pans and chill.
After it has thoroughly chilled you can slice it and fry it up.
Also it may be put into slices to freeze for later use.

NOTE: Be advised that the goetta will be more dry than the commercial goetta and will crumble more. This is due to the lower fat in the finished product. It is easier to digest and better for goetta dishes like goetta burritos etc.

HOMEMADE CHILI:
OHIO STYLE AND CINCINNATI

My husband Ed is a genuine soup and chili lover. One of our first dates in fact was to the a chili parlor in Clifton near the University of Cincinnati. This is a great gathering place for "UC" students over the years and one of several chains of "chili parlors" which dish up the "secret recipes" for the famous "Greek" style chili.

When you live in the area you tend to go and eat in these restaurants as they are close and reasonably priced — however, when you move from Ohio and you get the desire for a steaming "3-way," this recipe is the best. If you are not in a "chili parlor" in Southwest Ohio and you are in a general eatery of some kind you will find a pretty standard "Ohio" or "Midwestern" chili. I have started with this one. Great to serve in a bowl with macaroni or alone on cold winter days, and especially good when we have a snowstorm and everything shuts down. In over 25 years of marriage we have eaten a lot of chili.

Ed is one of those people who says 'I can fix it"... it is such a gift to have someone like that around! Having two chili recipes you too will be able to say: As far as chili is concerned — "I can fix it!"

HOMEMADE OHIO CHILI

1 ½ lbs ground sirloin (hamburger is too greasy, go for the
best meat you can afford) OR 1 lb vegetarian chub
1 (15 oz) can diced tomatoes
1 (15 oz) can tomato sauce
4 Tblsp worchestershire sauce
4 Tblsp brown sugar
4 Tblsp barbeque sauce
*Optional: 1 (14 oz) can red beans: drained

TOPPINGS:
½ cup chopped green pepper
½ cup chopped celery
½ cup chopped onion

SPICES:
2 Tblsp chili powder
1 Tblsp ground mustard
2 Tblsp hot sauce
1 teasp ground black pepper
1 teasp garlic powder

1. Brown ground sirloin.
2. Add tomatoes, sauce, worchestershire sauce,
   brown sugar, barbeque sauce (*Opt. add beans here)
3. Add spices and stir.
4. Simmer for 30-40 min. Stirring from time to time
5. Serve topped with chopped peppers, celery, onions
*You can also serve topped with shredded cheddar cheese.

RECIPES USING CHILI:

Chili Mac:
A real crowd pleaser. For this you cook separately a ½ box of elbow macaroni according to directions.
Then place in bowl and top with chili and cheese.

NOTE: This pot of chili will serve about 8-10 more
if you make up the macaroni.

There are no onions in this chili recipe—however IF you want onions in your chili you have the following options:
1. Chop and cook onions with the ground sirloin
    in the beginning.
2. Add raw onions to the green pepper /celery topping
    at serving.

Eggs Ranchero:
Make scrambled eggs.
Top with the Homemade Chili and grated cheddar cheese.
This recipe I picked up on one of my trips to the Southwest.
Serve with "texas" toast or on a flour tortilla.
Trim with sliced jalapeños if you dare!

Traditional Coney Islands/Chili Cheese Dogs:

Make hot dogs.

Spread mustard and chopped onions on the buns.

Put the hot dogs in the buns, and top with the chili and grated cheddar cheese.

You can eat these in quantity—so watch out!

South of the Border:

Put a handful of Corn chips on a plate.

(If you are really lazy- open up a snack bag of corn chips.)

Heat the chili and pour over the chips.

Top with grated cheddar cheese.

CINCINNATI-STYLE CHILI

Truthfully, no one except maybe 10 people in Cincinnati know the REAL recipe for this dish. This is another of those "passed around" copies. I think it is pretty good and if you are living out of town it is really good in a pinch if you are having a "chili-attack" and there is no "Chili Parlor" just down the street.

It does come from Greek and Macedonian immigrants and is close to the sauce which is used in many of their traditional dishes like "pastitcio." *I have made "pastitcio" with this chili as the meat sauce and it was wonderful!*

2 Tblsp garlic powder
4 Tblsp chili powder
1 Tblsp cinnamon
1 Tblsp dried red peppers
2½ teasp cumin
1 (8 oz) can tomato sauce
1½ Tblsp white vinegar
1 Tblsp worchestershire sauce
1 quart of water
2½ lbs lean ground beef
3 large onions left whole

SPICE BAG:
5 bay leaves
35 whole all spice

For extra-hot chili: Add 4 red peppers
(Spice bags are made with cheese cloth or
you can use an old tea ball)

1. Place all ingredients in a soup pot.

2. Cook at least 4 hours on low.

Serve the following ways:
1 way : Chili alone with crackers
2 way : Chili served over spaghetti.
3 way: Chili, spaghetti, and grated cheddar cheese on top
4 way: Chili, spaghetti, cheese and onions (you can
        substitute red beans for the onions for a 4 way Bean)
5 way: Chili, spaghetti, cheese, onions AND beans

Also good for Cheese Coneys:
Hot Dogs on buns with the buns prepared with mustard and
onions and then the Cincinnati-Style Chili is put over them

MOCK TURTLE SOUP
ALSO KNOWN AS: GERMAN CHILI

On really cold days growing up it was a "given" at home that your could either open up a can or, if you were in Cincinnati, go to a German restaurant in Over-The-Rhine and get real homemade Mock Turtle Soup. This is a genuine local delicacy. No turtles will be killed in the making of this soup!

Originally the soup was made from all sorts of strange left-overs like beef hearts and heads and likely a few hoofs as well. Today we have streamlined this process and made things incredibly easy. I have worked up even a "lo-cal" version – without any meat using the vegetarian beef substitute. The best meat however is still "hamburger"!!

Thoughts about Mock Turtle Soup:
Hooray for Turtles, may they live long and be happy!

* Optional sugar: If finished soup is too tart add granulated sugar to soup and cook 1 minute before serving.

NOTES: This soup really freezes poorly – we tried freezing it once and the eggs became like rubber in the soup so that was a one time event.

* This soup is a great appetizer for a traditional German meal and is still served in many fine German restaurants before the main course.

NOT REALLY (MOCK) TURTLE SOUP

SERVES ABOUT 10

1 ½ to 2 lbs ground beef
OR 1 pkg hamburger substitute (vegetarian)
Browned and drained (pre-cook both kinds)

1 cup ketchup
1 cup worchestershire sauce
½ a sliced lemon
½ a large onion, chopped

1 quart water
2 hardboiled eggs
15 hard gingersnap cookies soaked in water
1 Tblsp brown sugar
*Optional ¼ cup granulated sugar : for very sour lemons
  or sour soup

1. Put all of the ingredients except the eggs and gingersnap
   cookies in a large soup pot.
   Cook covered at a medium simmer for about 30 minutes.
2. Put gingersnap cookies in a bowl and soak with about
   ½ cup of water. Breakup as they soften and stir. It will
   look like a brown paste.
3. Add the gingersnap paste and the chopped hardboiled
   eggs to the soup pot.
4. Reduce heat and simmer another 30 minutes.
   Watch out, it will thicken up, so be prepared to add
   water to it to thin it up a bit.

THE CINCINNATI "SLIDER"

What can you say about ex-Cincinnatians who bond together to send for boxes and boxes of little frozen hamburgers to be sent to them in places like – Arizona?? What is interesting is that for years and years the "secret" recipe has been floating around the area and shhhhhhh... now YOU are in on it!!! This is an easy one and slightly lower fat than the original. These aren't the real WHITE CASTLES, but they sure are good!

1 lb ground sirloin
1 egg
½ pkg dried onion soup mix
hamburger sliced dill pickles
1 pkg large dinner rolls (sliced)
*Optional 4-5 slices of American cheese

1. Preheat oven to 325°
2. Mix the ground sirloin, egg and onion soup mix.
3. Spread out this mixture on a cookie sheet.
4. BEFORE baking: take a knife and cut out "sliders" about the size of the buns. Pre-cutting makes it easier to move the sliders when they are done.
   Top with American cheese.
5. Bake for 25 minutes.
6. Remove from oven and put on buns with 1-2 slices of the dill pickle chips.

NOTE:

I use ground sirloin to lower the amount of fat in this recipe—
IF you use ground beef or ANY other kind of beef your
burgers will be swimming in grease when you remove them
from the oven and you will have to drain them on paper
towels. This just helps you to make them and serve them
quickly and almost grease free. These taste amazingly like
the ones you remember eating years ago!

©2010 White Castle Management Co.

THE CINCINNATI BURGER!

While we are on the subject of hamburgers lest we forget the fact that in Cincinnati and vicinity some of the most famous hamburgers are made with tartar sauce or mayonnaise. This is a local "thing," as no matter where I have traveled have I ever seen "tartar sauce" or mayonnaise as — burger condiments.

Where did we get those burgers?
Frisch's, Carter's Drive-In, and the Red Barn!

Thinking about that GREAT taste of tartar sauce on hamburgers — there are several knockoff recipes flying around for a CINCINNATI HAMBURGER PIZZA.

Burger Sauce*
2 Tblsp mayonnaise
2 Tblsp ketchup
2 Tlbsp pickle relish
dash of yellow mustard

© 2008 Frisch's Restaurants, Inc. All Rights Reserved.

CINCINNATI HAMBURGER PIZZA

1 lb ground beef or ground chuck
1 pizza crust- this may be home-made
(the best ones are- or premade)
1 jar tartar sauce (or mayonnaise or burger sauce*)
4-5 slices American cheese
1 small jar hamburger dill pickle slices
½ head iceberg lettuce

1. Brown and drain ground meat.
   *Optional: while browning you can add 1 Tblsp of dried onions if you choose.
2. Make or open pizza crust and put in pan.
3. Top pizza with ground beef and the cover with American cheese slices.
4. Bake according to directions for your pizza crust. (about 8- 12 minutes)
5. Remove from oven and slightly cool.
6. Top with chopped lettuce, pickle slices and dollops of sauce.

Cincinnati BBQ

There are many notable BBQ "joints"– I mean restaurants –
in the greater Cincinnati area. There are local rivalries as well.
Gone is the F&N Steakhouse, while The Silver Spring House
and the Montgomery Inn live on to this day as places to get
great Ohio BBQ. Depending on your taste you may use any
BBQ sauce for the following recipe.

A "sweet" bbq sauce would be the best, however, created by
adding 1 teaspoon of sugar to any bbq sauce you do select.

© 2009 Montgomery Inn

BARBEQUE CHICKEN PIZZA

1 pre-made pizza crust (or homemade pizza crust)
½ cup diced cooked chicken
½ green pepper
½ cup chopped red onions
½ cup barbeque sauce
½ cup mozzarella cheese

1. Preheat oven according to pizza crust.
2. Top crust with chicken, green pepper, red onions.
*   Optional: chopped black olives may be added.
3. Drip barbeque sauce over the pizza and top with mozzarella cheese.
4. Bake according to crust directions.

This is another great party snack!!

POGUE'S DEPARTMENT STORE

The Camargo Room in Pogue's department store in downtown Cincinnati was at one time considered one of the BEST 'tea rooms" in the city and a great place for lunch! As a teen model, for nearby Mabley and Carew, I remember grabbing a quick lunch there. My "favs" were their salad with the "signature" French dressing and their "mulligatawny soup" (I have yet to find a recipe for it!)

Pogue's is no longer at the corner of Fourth and Race — now the Tower Place is there. The memories live on about meeting friends "on the go" for lunch and nicknaming the place "the Camaro Room" after the fast car! A very yellowed card shows that this has been in the file a long, long time . This recipe was requested many times in THE CINCINNATI ENQUIRER and I also understand it was given out on television as well. For old times sake— and without our white gloves— here is the classic dressing.

H.S. Pogue Company™ Associated Dry Goods™ 1962

POGUE'S FRENCH SALAD DRESSING

MAKES ABOUT 2 CUPS

½ cup ketchup
½ cup sugar
⅓ cup vegetable oil
⅓ cup wine vinegar
2½ Tblsp grated onions
½ teasp each:
paprika, chili powder, salt, dry mustard and celery seed

Combine all of the above ingredients and blend well.

To make dressing thicker: add more ketchup

To make thinner: add more vinegar and / or oil

©2010 THE CINCINNATI ENQUIRER

THE HOTEL SINTON

I learned to make this salad from a former member of the Hotel Sinton's culinary staff. Mrs. Brown was the dietary manager at Memorial Community Center where I got my first public relations job after college. Mrs. Brown had worked at the Hotel Sinton kitchen and "learned her craft" in the glory days of that grand hotel. The Spring Pea Salad was one of the recipes from that era. She recreated this salad for a luncheon at the Center in the 1970's which was hosted for local officials including the Mayor of Cincinnati Jerry Springer!

My Uncle Chris was a big band orchestra leader in Cincinnati. During the 1930's he played the roof garden of the Hotel Sinton with his dance music broadcast on a weekly program on WCIN radio. "Under the stars in beautiful Cincinnati from the roof garden of the Hotel Sinton..."

HOTEL SINTON'S SPRING PEA SALAD

2 (16 oz) bags frozen green peas
6 green onions: chopped.
2 stalks of celery: chopped fine
2 cups mayonnaise (more or less to suit taste)
4 hard boiled eggs: sliced

* This is best a "make ahead salad" to create the night
  before serving – or at least 6 hours prior to dinner.

RUSH SALAD:
Thaw peas in cold running water and then use.

1. Mix peas, onions and celery
2. Mix in 1 cup mayonnaise
3. Put in a 9 x 13 dish and top with 1 cup mayonnaise
4. Garnish with the hardboiled eggs
5. Serve. May be served over chopped lettuce

CINCINNATI DELICATESSENS

If you were always on the run in Cincinnati in the 1960's and 70's you knew "Izzy Kadetz's on Elm" or "The Temple on 7th" across from Shillito's department store. Great sandwiches, soups and amazing potato pancakes. Always crowded but quick service and you could always get things "to go." I am not sure if that is where my Uncle Chris got the "fatal" limburger cheese sandwich or not — by "fatal" — I will explain.

Uncle Chris Christensen was a noted big band musician and vibraharpist. He was always "on the go." One fateful evening he decided to pick up a limburger cheese and bermuda onion sandwich on rye. Unfortunately, he ate two bites and then jamming it back in the bag, left it in the car while he went on to his "gig." Getting off late, he next came home and went to bed. It was early summer. The next morning Aunt Marno went to take the car out and opening the car door smelled this terrible odor.

She started swearing that something had gotten in the car and died. Now this was no ordinary car but the "dream car" for this couple— the Mercedes with the leather upholstery. Thus became the next odyssey of cleaning for this car. Eventually they sold the car still with vague traces of the limburger cheese smell. The Temple, Uncle Chris and Aunt Marno and the Mercedes are all gone but the recipe for potato pancakes lives on.

© 2008 Izzy's

POTATO PANCAKES DELI-STYLE

These go great with corned beef or reuben sandwiches!

2 cup grated potatoes (drain and dry on paper towels)*
2 eggs (3 eggs for moister pancakes)
¼ cup chopped onions
2 Tblsp flour
1 Tblsp salt
½ teasp parsley
¼ teasp ground black pepper
vegetable oil

1. Grate and dry the potatoes.
2. Beat the eggs about 1 minute.
3. Add the potatoes, onion, flour, parsley, salt, pepper.
4. Heat in a skillet about ¼ inch oil for frying
5. Drop ¼ cup of the potato mix into the hot oil
6. Fry each side to a light golden brown.
7. Drain on paper towels before serving.
8. Serve with applesauce and sour cream.

You can also use pre-grated hash browns sold at the grocery

CINCINNATI APPLE TART FRANCAIS

This is not from one of our historic French restaurants however
— every time I serve this people ask — if it is the one which
they served! It is a very similar recipe to the famous Tarte
Aux Pommes once served at the late great Maisonette
Restaurant. This recipe is from a former neighbor who is
a native Parisian and is still living in Paris.

Sylvie invited me for "café" one afternoon and served this
magnificent apple tart — of course she did make the entire tart
crust and all. I have short cut this using "puff pastry." This is a
quick and really impressive dessert and incredibly simple.
Bon Appetit!

APPLE TART FRANCAIS

1 sheet frozen puff pastry
2 large apples
3 Tblsp each granulated sugar and brown sugar
1 Tblsp cinnamon
¼ stick butter

1. Thaw the puff pastry.
2. Peel and slice paper thin the apples.
3. Arrange the apples to cover the puff pastry.
4. Thinly slice the butter over the apples.
5. Sprinkle with both sugars and cinnamon.
6. Bake in a 350° oven according to puff pastry directions about 18 min. Lightly brown- be careful to not over cook!
7. Serve warm with ice cream.

Shillito's® Tea Room

One of the most famous of the tearooms in Cincinnati was in the Shillito's Dept Store at 7th and Race. Likely if you were going to eat downtown in a "tea room" it would be in either Pogues, Mc Alpins or Shillito's. These were THE tearooms in Cincinnati in the 1950's and 60's. I spent a lot of time in the Shillito Tea Room— I did some modeling as a teenager there, and I also was an "alternate" Suzy Snowflake there one year and ate many happy lunches there with my Aunt Marno.

My aunt didn't have any children so often her relatives and friends with children became her surrogate grandchildren at the Shillito Tea Room. One such noon one of those dear children, "Heather Anne" went completely into the cracker gumming and throwing the silverware mode in the elegant tea room. Aunt Marno, non-plussed by this, ordered dessert. In the meantime– Heather Anne continued to throw silverware– one of which–an ice tea spoon landed into her diaper bag! This went home with them to the later mortification of her mother- who had asked for an ice tea spoon during lunch when it seemed that one had not been placed on the table! (more mortification!) Thankfully after this episode, Heather Anne did not go into a life of crime.

From those many happy lunches at Shillito's where Allison only crumpled crackers and did not throw spoons, I have located from two sources the famous Shillito's 7 Hills BBQ Sandwich.

This I understand has also been published in the Cincinnati Enquirer and is NOT in the famous (and now out of print) Lazarus® Department Store Cookbook.

7 HILLS BAR-B-Q SANDWICH

1 ¼ lbs ground beef (or 1 lb vegetarian chub)
¼ cup diced onion
⅛ cup diced green pepper
½ Tblsp dry mustard
½ Tblsp cider vinegar
¾ cup ketchup
1 Tblsp sugar
salt and pepper

1. Brown ground beef over medium heat, stirring to break into small pieces, with onion and green pepper.
2. Stir in mustard, vinegar, ketchup and sugar.
3. Cook over low heat 30 minutes or until liquid is reduced as desired.
4. Salt and pepper to taste.
5. Serve on cheddar cheese buns
   (or top with grated cheddar cheese on an onion bun.)

Shillito's® / Lazarus® registered trademarks of Federated Department Stores,Inc.
© 2010 THE CINCINNATI ENQUIRER

THE BLACK COW / THE PINK COW

From 1950 through 1985 the Uncle Al Show on Cincinnati's WCPO-TV, Channel 9 was the morning delight for many children of several generations in the Greater Cincinnati area.

Uncle Al, like many performers in his era, was the master of doing the "live show" with his accordion and lively songs, creative sets his lovely wife Wanda (Captain Windy) and "Lucky" the clown he had an audience who loved him and waited many months for tickets to come and see him in the WCPO studios in Cincinnati.

Uncle Al also was terrific with his "live" commercials which he did for a number of products each day with clever songs and jingles. Of all of these daily he taught his young audience how to make a "Black Cow" or a "Pink Cow" (there were a few other colors as well, purple, orange) with soft drinks.

The commercial break was always the same. Uncle Al or Captain Windy would sing a little song about the beverage company and then get into the live part about "how to make a black cow."

HOW TO MAKE A BLACK COW

1 tall glass
1 scoop of vanilla ice cream
1 bottle of Root Beer (black cow)
OR Crème Soda (pink cow)

1. Place scoop of ice cream in the tall glass.
2. Add the Root Beer.
3. Stir with a spoon
4. Drink with a straw.

UNCLE AL SHOW® WCPO-TV :
Scripps TV STATION GROUP © THE E.W. Scripps Company

CINCINNATI TV TREATS:
RUTH LYONS

When I mentioned I was working on this collection of "hometown" Cincinnati recipes to a friend and I mentioned how all the "moms" used to copy down her recipes from TV. As it turned out there were yellowing cards in her family recipe file as well. These were so popular with many families, that even today, some are still found on holiday and picnic tables around Cincinnati.

Ruth Lyons was remarkable. She was the first long running daytime talk show host on television. Her program the 50-50 Club on WLW-T in Cincinnati was seen in Cincinnati, Dayton, Columbus, Ohio Indianapolis, SW Indiana, Covington, Newport, Lexington Kentucky as well as parts of West Virginia I am told. Before cable television, this was unheard of for a non-national television program.

Ruth (a former radio organist) had a dry wit and a love of music which meant there was a "live band"—Cliff Lash and of course "live" singers—too numerous to mention. Her co-host was Bob Braun. Daily she had one of her assistants, Elsa Sule appear with some culinary treat. A lot of times the story goes it was something to do with peanut butter...however from time to time Ruth would share one of "her" recipes. It has always been questioned "whose" recipes these were, but for the sake of the faded and often used file cards in my box— I will say they ARE Ruth's. Here are the great gelatin salad and coffee cake recipes. Easy to make, enjoyed by many.

RUTH LYONS'

CRANBERRRY-CHERRY GELATIN

6 oz box cherry gelatin
1 can bing cherries: drained, juice reserved.
1 (15 oz) can whole cranberry sauce
½ cup chopped apple
½ cup chopped nuts
½ cup chopped celery (optional)

1. With the juice from the drained cherries add enough water to make 2 cups of liquid.
2. Heat to boiling and dissolve gelatin.
3. Cool slightly and fold in cherries, cranberry sauce, apples, chopped nuts, and celery.
4. Chill until firm.

Ruth Lyons' 50-50 Club © AVCO BROADCASTING CO. CINCINNATI, OHIO

COFFEE CAKE

I have seen several versions of this coffee cake. This I think is the best one and closest to the original. Again these were given "on the air" and copied down by the ladies at home.

1 cup sugar
1 cup brown sugar
2 ¾ cups flour
1 egg
1 cup milk
1 teasp vinegar
¾ cup vegetable oil
1 teasp baking soda
1 teasp each-cinnamon, nutmeg
1 teasp salt

1. Preheat oven to 350°
2. Mix together the sugar, brown sugar, flour, cinnamon, nutmeg and salt.
3. Add oil. Stir until crumbly.
4. Reserve and aside ¾ cup of mixture for topping.
5. Add vinegar to the milk and stir into the sugar mixture.
6. Add the egg and the soda and mix well.
7. Pour into a greased 13 x 9 inch pan.
8. Sprinkle with reserve topping.
9. Bake 30 min.

SOUP

FOR ALL TIMES

Old Fashioned Bean Soup	45
Old Fashioned Beef and Barley Soup	47
Easy Broccoli and Cheese Soup	49
Homemade Split Pea Soup	51
Blue Ribbon Tortellini Soup	53
White Chicken Chili	54

SEASONAL FAVORITES

SPRING: Steak Soup	57
SUMMER: Gazpacho	59
FALL: Pumpkin Soup	61
WINTER: Leftover Turkey Noodle Soup	63

TOMATO: THE KING OF SOUPS

CANNED TOMATO SOUP FAVORITES

Classic Tomato Soup : Cream of Tomato :	
Classic Tomato Rice : Tomato-Beef :	66
Double Tomato : Taco Tomato	67

INTERNATIONAL!

FRANCE: Chou Soup (Diet Cabbage Soup)   71

MEXICO: Easy Tortilla Soup   73

ITALY: Italian Market Soup   75

     White Bean and Pasta Soup   77

CARIBBEAN: Easy Black Bean Soup   79

CZECHOSLOVAKIA: Cabbage Soup   81

ASIAN: Easy Chinese Style Soup   83

HUNGARY: Not Your Mother's Goulash   85

     Crock Pot Goulash   86

QUICK SOUPS

Quick Soups With Ramen Noodles   88

Canned Soups As Bases   89

Soup for All Times

OLD FASHIONED BEAN SOUP

It is a cold and rainy winter day. Things have not gone well. It is a comfort to know that tomorrow the sun is supposed to shine. My Dad would always say "Every day is a new day" – that and a bowl of bean soup is the truth.

That is it. We are all the same. What was remarkable about my Dad is that he could "talk across" to everyone be it a doctor or a cashier. Friendliness and kindness to those you do not know. The ability to really get along. Dad loved beef and beans "Every day is a new day." Which was Dad's way of saying that each day we can turn over a new leaf and begin again. We can keep going. We can ride out the storm.

MAKES ABOUT 8-10 CUP SERVINGS

1 lb dried navy beans
½ cup chopped ham
½ cup chopped onion
½ cup chopped celery
1 cup instant mashed potatoes

SPICES:
1 bay leaf
1 Tblsp garlic powder
1 Tblsp oregano
¼ teasp salt
¼ teasp black pepper

1. Rinse and sort beans.
2. Put beans in the soup pot and add enough water to cover. Bring to a boil. Cover pot and turn off burner. Let sit for one hour.
3. Add onions, celery and carrots plus 4 cups of water and spices. Return to a boil.
4. Simmer on medium for 2 hours, stirring from time to time.
5. Mash beans with a slotted spoon or potato masher. Add instant potatoes to thicken.
6. Serve with crackers and sprinkle with hot sauce

OLD FASHIONED BEEF & BARLEY SOUP

If there is a true comfort food, this is it. In our family this soup goes back so far that no one knows who made it first. People always remember eating it as kids during the "great depression" era when the soup was made with beef bones bought from the local butcher, which still works today. As a child I remember the brawls with the sibs for the "marrow bones" and putting the cooked beef marrows on crackers after fishing them out of the soup pot! I raised my daughter on the "millionaire's soup" using stew meat in the soup... although the bones still work.

There are no truly hard times but those which we accept as being "hard." It is our spirit and our positive attitude which keep us going in these times. "Waste not, want not" was a phrase my Mother used when we were kids. Using even the bones in the soup proved this lesson and reminded us to use everything possible.

Variations on the soup:
1. Use vegetable-tomato juice instead of water in the soup base.
2. Add worchestershire sauce to the soup about 3 Tblsp.
3. To save time: use frozen or canned mixed vegetables.

(Also known by our daughter, Allison as a child as "Happy Barley Soup"... look for the smiling barley!)

1 lb of ONE of the following:
BEEF: soup bones and meat OR lean leg beef OR stew meat
1 cup chopped onion
1 (28 oz) can of tomatoes
1 cup chopped celery
1 cup chopped carrots
6 cups water
4 beef bouillon cubes

SPICES:
½ teasp garlic salt
½ teasp salt
½ teasp black pepper
1 box of barley

1. Brown meat and onions in garlic salt in soup pan.
2. Add vegetables, water and spices.
3. Bring to a boil and simmer for 1 hour.
4. Add bouillon cubes.
5. In a separate pan cook barley according to directions.
6. Combine barley and soup and serve.

Cook and refrigerate the extra soup.
NOTE: It can be frozen and does freeze well.

EASY BROCCOLI & CHEESE SOUP

My Aunt Marno loved to eat and was an excellent cook. She also made Beef and Barley soup. One of her favorites eating out at restaurants, and particularly the old Pogue's department store Tea Room, was Broccoli-Cheese Soup.

But she also really loved the way that I made it. The only problem was that she didn't like chicken and never ate chicken. There is a chicken base in most broccoli cheese soup recipes and this one I make is no different. I never told my aunt it was in there and she loved this soup all the same.

Which brings me to the point that we should not ruin someone's happiness or joy unless it is absolutely necessary. Joy is fleeting, life is long. Even a bowl of soup in its momentary life should be enjoyed for the comfort it brings.

MAKES ABOUT 6-8 CUP SERVINGS

1 (10 oz) can cream of chicken soup
1 (10 oz) can cream of celery soup
1 ½ cups milk
1 (10 oz) pkg frozen chopped broccoli
1 cup cubed pasteurized prepared cheese product
1 (8 oz) bag finely shredded cheddar cheese

SPICES:
¼ teasp ground mustard
½ teasp garlic powder

1. Mix soups and milk and heat.
2. Cook separately broccoli according to package directions and drain.
3. Add broccoli and spices.
4. In a pyrex cup heat cubed cheese in microwave with 2 tablespoons of milk for 30-40 sec, or until softened. Mix with a spoon and add some soup to the cup.
5. Pour cheese mixture into soup and stir until smooth heating through.
6. Bring to a boil while stirring.
7. Serve with ⅛ cup of shredded cheese on top.

HOMEMADE SPLIT PEA SOUP

It was Allison, my daughter, who was the inspiration and a major "soup eater" at home who requested I DO this collection of home style, "Ohio" style recipes for a friend of hers who loved soup. When I asked for her thoughts about this book she immediately endorsed the "Happy Barley" soup recipe...so I guess that one is going to go on to another generation! But her second favorite is Homemade Split Pea Soup.

Allison always lights up a room with her happy personality and ready smile. So when the seasons are changing and you have a little left over Christmas or Easter ham and the rain and wind have got you thinking summer will never get here—think of a lovely day and a happy smile.

Idea! Joy is with you every day. You carry it IN you.

3 cups dried split peas
½ cup ham bits OR ham bone
1 small onion: chopped
½ cup celery: chopped
½ cup carrots: chopped
6 cups water

SPICES:
1 teasp garlic powder
½ teasp oregano
½ teasp black pepper

1. Rinse and sort peas.
2. Put peas and all ingredients in soup pan. Bring to a boil.
3. Simmer on low heat about 2 hours.
    Stirring from time to time.
4. Soup will thicken. May be thinned with additional water,
    or thickened with instant mashed potatoes.

Serve topped with croutons.

NOTES:
Cut-up potatoes can also be added to this soup as well as
greater amounts of cooked ham.

OHIO 4H FAVORITES

I think that I would likely never have tried either of these two recipes if it weren't for 4H. Since 1997, I have been affiliated with Ohio 4H as a club advisor, judge and county key advisor. Over this time I have been to many county fairs and of course the ever popular and in the heat of the summer Ohio State Fair.

Allison made soup for cooking project at our local Warren County Ohio Fair one year and won a blue ribbon for it. I am not sure where the original recipe came for it but it is still a "wow" today and definitely a "first class" soup! 4Hers all know that "You are a winner by doing— even if you don't get first place!" So make this soup and enjoy—even though this time you will not be awarded the "blue ribbon" except by maybe your family.

Also "White Chicken Chili" another popular 4H club favorite.

BLUE RIBBON TORTELLINI SOUP

4 cans chicken broth
1 cup frozen peas
1 cup shredded carrots
½ cup chopped celery
½ cup chopped onion
½ (19 oz) bag frozen tortellini
½ bag (10 oz) chopped spinach (cooked and drained)
parmesan cheese (shaker style)

SPICES:
½ teasp dried parley, garlic powder and oregano

1. Combine all ingredients except spinach and tortellini in soup pan.
2. Simmer 30 minutes.
3. Add tortellini to soup.
4. Cook spinach according to directions making sure to drain it.
5. Serve mixing in the cooked spinach with each serving. Top with parmesan cheese.

NOTES:
Does not freeze too well as the tortellini can get mushy.
ADD Spinach LAST. If you forget and put it in the soup before the end of the soup cooking process the soup will turn green and look terrible. It will taste fine- just look bad.

WHITE CHICKEN CHILI

SERVES ABOUT 4 PEOPLE

3 cans chicken broth
½ chopped onion
3 cooked and diced chicken breasts
OR 3 packages (8 oz) of cooked chicken
1 4 oz can green chilies chopped
½ cup frozen pepper stir-fry mix
1 teasp garlic powder
1 ½ teasp black pepper
dash hot sauce
¼ cup fresh cilantro chopped
grated cheddar cheese: to top
*Optional: 1 can Great Northern beans

1. Saute onion
2. Add all ingredients (except cheese)
3. Simmer 20 min.
4. Serve with cheese on top.

SEASONAL FAVORITES

SPRING

There is nothing like the cold rainy and sometimes very unpredictable Ohio spring. No matter what the groundhog says there are always 6 more weeks of winter after February 2. One way or another we have at least 4 more snows on any given year. It can freeze going into May. These are givens. So when it comes to soup you have to think of something which will make people feel cheered up in this weird weather and enjoy coming in out of the rain, sleet or snow for a nice bowl of soup.

Thoughts about Spring:
It will stop raining!
Don't you just love those daffodils?
Think it's hot now- just wait until August!

A year round favorite at our house has been something called "Steak Soup." This is one of many variations of this dish. I will even add details for the vegetarian version which I also often make.

STEAK SOUP

1 ½ lbs lean ground beef OR 1 chub veggie protein
½ cup chopped carrots
½ cup chopped celery
1 can diced tomatoes
4 cups water
4 chicken bouillon cubes
½ cup chopped mushrooms
2 Tblsp dried, minced onions
*Optional: 1 pkg noodles

THICKENING:
Use margarine melted with 2 Tblsp flour

SPICES:
1 Tblsp garlic powder
2 Tblsp worchestershire sauce
2 Tblsp pepper sauce
1 teasp ground black pepper

1. In soup pan, brown meat and drain.
2. Add all veggies (except mushrooms) and cook on
   low heat for 5 minutes to soften them.
3. Heat the water separately and dissolve bouillon cubes.
4. Add to soup pot (or use canned chicken broth instead)
5. Add spices, mushrooms and onions.
6. Cover and simmer 20 minutes.
7. Thicken using margarine/flour (roue) with broth.
8. Cook noodles according to the package.
9. Serve soup over noodles.

SUMMER

After what seems like an eternity summer finally comes around and it gets hot...usually really hot. We are talking 90 to 100 degrees at times. Good for being on the lazy side.

Cooling off at the Great Lakes or the pool or cruising down the Ohio River, soup is about the very last thing you might think of but at our house a great favorite on those really hot days is a very cool bowl of easy homemade gazpacho.

Thoughts about summer:
You think it's hot here? Try Death Valley.
You will wish for this day in January!

COOL HOMEMADE GAZPACHO

2-3 cups fresh tomatoes peeled and diced
OR use 1 (28 oz) can diced tomatoes
1 (46 oz) can tomato / vegetable juice
½ cup chopped bell pepper
½ finely chopped onion
1 cup diced cucumber

SPICES:
1 Tblsp garlic powder
1 teasp worchestershire sauce
1 teasp hot sauce
½ teasp ground black pepper
2 Tblsp lemon juice
2 Tblsp olive oil

1. Mix all ingredients in a large bowl.
2. Cover and refrigerate for 3 hours.
3. Serve garnished with rounds of cucumber on top

Autumn

It is wonderful to have our summer linger into September here in Ohio. But by mid-October the "summer" party is about over and the leaves are in their peak and the cool crisp nights remind us that winter is just around the corner.

In October every year— for over 100 years a little town in central Ohio, Circleville, has a festival which celebrates the pumpkin. It is one of the largest street fairs in the U.S. and loaded with pumpkin fritters, pumpkin butter, pumpkin waffles, you just name it!

We had this soup for the first time not at this favorite festival of ours — we try to go every year — but on a cruise ship in the middle of the Caribbean! This is a recipe for pumpkin soup which we like.

Thoughts about Autumn:
Take time to revel under the beautiful trees and blue skies.
Life is too short to not be enjoyed!

PUMPKIN SOUP

2 Tblsp minced garlic
2 Tblsp margarine
2 (14 oz) cans chicken broth (or vegetarian broth)
1 (15 oz) can pure pumpkin
Dash cinnamon
*Optional: sour cream or croutons

THICKENING:
2 Tblsp margarine
2 Tblsp flour

1. Saute garlic in the margarine .
2. Add to the soup pot, the chicken broth and the pumpkin.
3. Cook until heated through and comes to a boil,
   stirring so it doesn't burn.
4. In separate pan melt margarine and add flour.
   Thin with some of the soup.
   Add to the soup and stir.
5. When the soup is thickened serve.
6. Season with salt and pepper if desired.
7. If desired, top with sour cream and fresh made
   croutons when serving

WINTER

This is the difficult heading as we are mostly soup eaters all winter around here and there are many favorites at our house which could go under the "winter" heading. I thought about this and decided that with all the holidays there is likely a left-over turkey carcass hanging around...well in the refrigerator.

So a good one to nurse those cold symptoms and end the year with might be the ever popular and mostly winter season, Turkey Noodle Soup.

I have tried many versions of this soup but a few years back found one where a can of tomatoes is flung into it. This is particularly good. So here is my version of the soup (now improved) with tomatoes.

Thoughts for Winter:
You will wish for this day in July!
Wow! a snow day- let's make snow angels in the lawn
before work—maybe after work but let's DO it!!
Snow is so white and pure when it falls—
what a beautiful thing it is—from indoors

Great for those who are suffering the seasonal colds, flu and "bugs."

LEFTOVER TURKEY NOODLE SOUP

1 turkey carcass (leftover from Thanksgiving/Christmas etc.)
½ cup chopped celery
½ cup chopped carrots
2 Tblsp minced garlic
½ medium onion
1 large can (28 oz) diced tomatoes, drained
1 Tblsp oregano
1 Tblsp ground black pepper
3 Tbsp dried parsley
1 pkg noodles : with or without yolks
*2 chicken bouillon cubes

1. Pick off any excess turkey for other turkey recipes.
2. Depending on size of carcass- you may have to break it
   into pieces- put in stockpot.
   (A soup pot will not do on this occasion.)
3. Add to the turkey : the celery, carrots, onion, garlic and
   cover with water(This will be at least 1½ -2 quarts) so
   that there is at least 2-3 inches of water over the carcass.
4. Bring to a boil. Then simmer uncovered 2½ hours.
5. Pull the turkey carcass out of the soup. (Some people like to
   strain the soup at this point either way you have to take out the
   bones) Pick off any additional loose meat to add to the soup.
6. Add the parsley, oregano, pepper and the drained
   tomatoes return to a boil.
7. Add about 6-8 oz of the noodles and cook for an
   additional 10 minutes.

NOTE: If you feel that the turkey flavor is "weak" add the bouillon
cubes to the soup before serving. They will add a salty taste as
well. You will note there is no added salt in this recipe.

TOMATO: THE KING OF SOUPS

O.k. so this is a bit of a presumption. But asking most kids this is a great favorite. At our house with a toasty grilled cheese sandwich anytime of year...yum!

Now this classic we know best from a "can." So here are a bunch of "tomato versions" using canned tomato soup. Sure to please everyone in the family who loves this soup.

THOUGHTS ON TOMATO SOUP:
"This too will pass." No matter how good or how bad things are they will change.
"Youth is short, enjoy the time you have now."

THE JOY OF TOMATO SOUPS!

Classic Tomato Soup
Make as directed on the can.
1. 1 can of soup with one can of water.
2. Heat and serve. Makes about 2 bowls

Cream of Tomato Soup
Use milk in place of the water.
Top with croutons.

Classic Tomato Rice Soup
Use Classic Tomato Soup and add ½ C of cooked rice
*Optional : ½ C of stir fry pepper mix
  (cooked and added to the soup)

Tomato-Beef Soup
Classic Tomato Soup with ½ lb of browned and
drained ground beef added.

Double Tomato Soup

Classic Tomato Soup with 1 can (15 oz) diced tomatoes or for more flavor add 1can of stewed tomatoes chopped.

Taco Tomato Soup

Classic Tomato Soup with:
½ pkg dry Taco Seasoning
½ cup salsa
1 can (15 oz) chopped tomatoes
½ lb browned and drained ground beef
*Optional: ½ can red beans

Heat and serve.

Top with chopped onions, grated cheddar cheese, tortilla chips and a dab of sour cream

SOUP INTERNATIONAL!

FRANCE

The last time Allison and I were in France we had the great plea-
sure of dining with her former exchange family from the 5th grade.
The Fievezs of Moisseney. In the small town in Ohio where we
live: Lebanon, for a time some of the 5th graders went to France
for a few weeks and then some of the French children they stayed
with came here. No kidding. 5th graders. Since when Allison was
in 5th grade they have now opted to go to Space Camp instead
of France. France IS more interesting.

Anyway.. after all this time I finally got to go to France and meet
"la famille de Jessica" (Allison's exchange counterpart) I was
welcomed as visiting royalty with a marvelous french country meal
designed by "Grandmere" herself!...While at table, a family friend
Stephen, was trying his english out on me and declared he was
doing the "Chou Diet"... quickly it came to me that through the joy
and perplexity of the internet- he meant the ever popular and new
Cabbage Diet Soup and Diet plan as featured in many maga-
zines etc. This soup IS not french. I have a recipe which is some-
what modified too from the original I think- no one seems to know
WHICH recipe (if any) IS original. .. but it just goes to show that
worldwide even the french eat this very veggie and silly soup. So
to salute my friendship with many french people and my love for
France and their skinny black dresses...here is "chou soupe"...Ha!
They must BE on the "cabbage diet" to get into those dresses!

Thoughts on Chou Soupe:
C'est La Vie ! (That's life !)
C'est Si Bon! (That's good!)

CHOU SOUPE: DIET CABBAGE SOUP

SERVES 8-10

1 medium head cabbage: cored and chopped
1 medium onion: chopped
1 large green pepper: chopped
1 (28 oz) can diced tomatoes
1 cup carrot -julienned
1 (10 oz) container of fresh mushrooms sliced
1 (10 oz) pkg frozen cut green beans
4 beef bouillon cubes
1 (46 oz) can vegetable juice (like a V8)
2 Tblsp worchestershire sauce
2 Tblsp olive oil
2 Tblsp garlic powder

1. Cook onions in soup pot, in the olive oil.
2. Add green pepper, carrots and chopped cabbage along with the tomatoes (do not drain the tomatoes) and green beans.
3. Add the sliced mushrooms, worchestershire sauce and the vegetable juice. Stir in the garlic powder.
4. Add about 2 cups of water.
5. Bring to a boil and cook 1½ to 2 hours over medium heat.
6. Serve with salt and pepper to taste.

NOTES: Can be eaten morning -noon -or night for the diet.. although I think it is a bit hard to face that cabbage first thing in the a.m. You WILL have GAS as a bi-product of this soup... so if you take any preparation for gas be sure that having cabbage as the main ingredient this could be a concern.

MEXICO

I just love Mexico. The water is so blue there. The people are so friendly and the food is just amazing. Wow! To make another long story short this recipe is NOT from Mexico. A couple of years ago my neighbor, Diana and I spent considerable time looking for the "perfect" tortilla soup. Being a pastor's wife she has a ton of quality experience with potlucks and soup nights at her church. We tried a number of good recipes. Finally when I went to a local Mexican restaurant (which is now out of business) I thought I stumbled upon the perfect combinations. And it turned out to be easy... and even better, everyone loved it, including my great friend Judy the English professor.

Thoughts on Tortilla Soup:
Always remember something "fun" can at times actually be good for you. Ole!
I can only imagine Antonio Banderas eating this for lunch—ha ha. Not.

EASY TORTILLA SOUP

2 (10 oz) cans chicken with rice soup
½ cup medium salsa
¼ cup chopped fresh cilantro (optional)
½ cup crispy corn tortilla chips
¼ cup finely shredded cheddar cheese
2 Tblsp sour cream

1. Mix the soup with 2 soup cans of water.
2. Add the salsa and the cilantro.
3. Heat to boiling
4. Spoon into dishes and put some chips in each bowl.
5. Top the chips with the cheese and top that with the sour cream.

NOTES:
This can be made up at a moment's notice for a crowd.

ITALY

I will always think fondly of my days spent in Italy and of eating Italian food...what wonderful food I have enjoyed in that beautiful country.. hence the "inspiration" for these 2 soups. No they are not from Italy but they have their roots there. The marketplace is the "hub" of most cities in Europe and even today the outdoor markets flourish. I have wandered through these in Rome and remember fondly of the charming markets and shops in Pisa where I like to think that my "market soup" with all of it's vegetables could be made. This soup was a favorite of my in-laws, Ed and Lois, and I am told that on the last day of her life, Lois ate this soup for her very last meal. A compliment for certain!

Thoughts about Market Soup:
There is some- thing warm and friendly in everyone...
but you sometimes have to look for it.

ITALIAN MARKET SOUP

SERVES ABOUT 4-5

1 (26 oz) can tomato soup
1 (14 oz) can diced tomatoes
1 (16 oz) bag frozen Italian-style vegetables
½ cup chopped onions
3 Italian sausages: sliced, diced (precooked)
1 cup ditalini pasta

SEASON TO TASTE:
Oregano leaves, black pepper, garlic powder

1. Mix tomato soup and water and tomatoes
2. Microwave Italian veg. and onions 4 minutes
3. Cook pasta according to package
4. Add vegetables to soup with sausage bits and pasta
5. Cook 15 minutes
6. Add ½ teasp oregano.
   Black pepper and garlic powder to taste.
7. Cook 5 min more
8. Serve topped with parmesan cheese

SOUP INTERNATIONAL!
More from Italy

In writing this one down, I remember my neighbor Moira liked this one. Moira thought about making it as a low-salt dish which was a good idea. So for this version we will do it her way. Moira is incredibly smart, she always won at party games and everyone wanted to be her partner.

Thoughts on White Bean Soup:
It is great to remember and always cherish our friends whether they are next door or many miles away. They are the special people who are in our lives by choice.

WHITE BEAN & PASTA SOUP

1 (15 oz) can Great Northern Beans
3 cup low salt chicken broth- this can be canned
OR your own chicken stock broth
1 cup "no salt" tomatoes
½ teasp oregano leaves
½ cup ditilani or small elbow macaroni pasta
½ cup shaved carrots
½ cup chopped celery
1 teasp garlic powder
grated parmesan cheese

1. Combine broth, beans, tomatoes, oregano and the carrots and celery.
2. Boil. Reduce heat and simmer about 5 min.
3. Stir in pasta and cook about 8-7 more min. until the pasta is done.
4. Serve topped with parmesan cheese.

NOTES:
This soup is vegetarian however if you want it to have more substance you can add some chopped leftover cooked ham to the pot.

CARIBBEAN

The lilt of the steel drums, the beautiful sunsets over the Bahamas or Jamaica and the tropical warm breezes filled with the scent of fragrant flowers easily put you in the mood on a winter's day for the tropics. My familiarity with the "black bean" started in the 1990's when I was in the Bahamas consuming Fried Conch and "Peas and Rice".

The "peas" looking an awful lot like our "black beans" at home. The recipes for Caribbean Black bean soup I have made come from many places. I tried one a few years ago which was reputedly served at the Kentucky Derby, which is in Kentucky and nowhere near the Caribbean. The recipe which follows is a composite of several I have tried over the years and which works for me. The family likes it too.

Thoughts about Caribbean Black Bean Soup:
Life is short- Don't Worry So!
Smile and the sun will shine!

EASY BLACK BEAN SOUP

2 cans black beans
(this makes it easy as the beans are already pre-cooked)
½ medium onion chopped
½ teasp dried minced garlic
2 Tblsp olive oil
1 (15 oz) can stewed tomatoes
½ teasp cayenne pepper
1 teasp dried chicken bouillon
½ cup sour cream
croutons

OPTIONAL:
½ teasp dry sack sherry
½ cup cooked ham bits
½ cup instant rice or cooked rice

1. Cook onions and garlic together in oil.
2. Add beans (undrained) and stewed tomatoes.
3. Add spices (and the ham if you add it).
4. Simmer 20 min.
5. Mash some of the beans. Add the instant rice and simmer another 10 minutes.
6. Serve: Mixing the sherry into each serving and topping with the sour cream and croutons.

CZECHOSLOVAKIA

Just when you thought that we had done it with Chou soup out pops another cabbage creation. I am convinced that much of Europe functions on cabbage . This is a recipe which I have made in a number of variations. My father's family is from Slovakia where cabbage soups are a tradition. This is a hearty soup which is easy to make and is generally well liked. It is especially good in the winter. For Lent it is made without the sausage.

Thoughts about Cabbage Soup:
It is a great comfort to know that some things go from generation to generation. From country to country we eat soup and connect to our past and to those we have never met.

CABBAGE SOUP

4 cup shredded cabbage
4 cup water
1 small onion chopped
3 teasp garlic salt
½ cup carrots chopped
½ to 1 polska kiebasa sausage (1 lb) sliced thin pieces
(OR smoked sausage)
*Optional: instant potato flakes

1. Brown sausage in skillet in 1 Tbsp vegetable oil.
2. Add all ingredients to the soup pot.
3. Boil 10 min. and then simmer without lid for 1 ½ hours.
4. Thicken with flour and water or instant potato flakes.
5. Serve. Season with salt and pepper.

NOTES:
Can be served with noodles.
Soup can be made without sausage and topped
with crisp bacon.

SOUP INTERNATIONAL!

ASIA

One of the great things about going to dinner at chinese restaurants is the delicious soups they begin the meals with. They always seems to be "light" and really are a great start to the dinner. Some are almost "diet" food, in fact a chinese student of mine, Janet, gave me some chicken bouillon cubes as a "diet" secret from China. It seems that there if you want to lose a few pounds you just have a cup of bouillon before the meal and you will reduce your calorie intake.

I enjoy chinese style favors and the addition of fresh peapods and bean sprouts in the soup so here is a "chinese style" soup right from an American kitchen

Wisdom from Chinese Style Soup:
Tranquillity is good.
True beauty can be found in nature.

CHINESE STYLE SOUP

3 chicken bouillon cubes
½ medium onion: sliced very thin
½ cup fresh mushrooms: sliced very thin
½ cup fresh bean sprouts (mung- the larger ones)
½ cup fresh pea pods
½ teasp soy sauce
*Optional: ½ cup cooked rice

1. Heat 4 cups of water to a boil.
2. Add only the vegetables above and simmer for 10 minutes.
3. Add the bouillon cubes and dissolve.
4. Add soy sauce.
5. Return to boil, add cooked rice before serving.

HUNGARY

There is always one thing for sure when you talk to Hungarians and that is their family has the "original" goulash recipe. OK. I have been making various goulash recipes for years having a husband who is half Hungarian we certainly have tried many "new ones."

This is traditionally served with noodles and definitely is "soupy" even without being considered a true "soup." I am going to include here my "favorite" recipes at the moment — there is sure to be another to try next week ! I have a stove top version and a "crock pot" one.

Thoughts about Goulash:
There is always a reason to go home.
Even on a truly bad day goulash will make things seem better.

NOT YOUR MOTHER'S GOULASH

SERVES ABOUT 3-4½ CUP SERVINGS

1 ½ -2 lbs beef : stew, top round steak: lean meat
2 Tblsp olive oil
1 medium onion sliced thin
1 Tblsp garlic powder
2 Tblsp paprika
1 can tomato paste
2 cup water
2 beef bouillon cubes
½ teasp black pepper
½ cup sour cream

1. Saute the onions in the olive oil .
2. Add the garlic and the beef and paprika.
3. Browning the beef add about ½ cup water and simmer
   on low for about 20 minutes.
4. Add the 2 cup water and the 2 beef bouillon cubes
   dissolved in it and the tomato paste.
5. Cover and simmer about 40 minutes or until meat is tender.
6. At serving time add: ½ cup sour cream

Variations:
Add : 1 sliced green pepper
        1 sliced tomato or small can diced tomatoes.
This version can cook as long as 2 hours.

CROCK POT GOULASH

Really Slow...

1 ½ lbs stew / lean beef cuts
1 Tbsp olive oil
1 can cream of mushroom soup
1 cup water
½ teasp seasoned salt
1 medium potato: diced
1 medium carrot: diced
½ medium onion: diced and sauted
8 fresh mushrooms: sliced

1. Brown meat in olive oil and onions.
2. Put everything else in the crock pot.
3. Cook 8 hours
4. Add ½ cup sour cream before serving.

Serve over noodles or spaetzle.

Suggestions for serving sides include:
Homemade bread
Sweet Sour Cucumber Salad
Pickled Red Beets

TIME FOR QUICK SOUP

This category is the one most often you may turn to.
No one seems to have any time to make soup every week.
These are some super quick combos to help you when
you find you want soup and are running on the fast track.

INSTANT THOUGHTS FOR QUICK SOUPS:
Kindness is free! You can be kind as quickly as being unkind.
One kind word can change someone's day for the better.

Call a friend. It takes a moment to "keep in touch".
Make it a policy to telephone an older friend or senior.
This is a great connection for them and for you.
Remember: This WILL be YOU someday!

QUICK SOUPS WITH RAMEN NOODLES

Chicken Based Ramen Noodles:

Add to: 2 packs Chicken Ramen Noodles: cooked
and 2 cups of water
½ pkg frozen stir-fry vegetables: cooked

OR

Add to: 2 packs Chicken Ramen Noodles: cooked
and 2 cups of water
½ pkg frozen pea pods: cooked
½ pkg fresh mushrooms: steamed (4 oz)

Beef Based Ramen Noodles:

Add to one pack Beef based Noodles:
1 large can (46 oz) Tomato-Vegetable Juice
1 pkg frozen mixed vegetables
2 Tblsp worchestershire sauce

Cook 10 minutes.

CANNED SOUPS AS BASES

Quick Spinach Soup

1 can cream of chicken soup (with 1 can milk)
½ cup cooked rice
½ cup frozen spinach

1. Heat through, chicken soup, milk and rice.
2. Add ½ cup of frozen spinach.
3. Heat and serve.

Quick Homemade Clam Chowder

1 can cream of potato soup (with 1 can milk)
1 can minced clams (drain off ½ liquid)
¼ cup chopped onions
¼ cup chopped celery
garlic powder to taste

1. Saute onions and celery in 1 Tblsp oil in a skillet.
2. Add everything in a soup pot.
3. Heat through and then serve.

EASTSIDE-WESTSIDE DESSERT

All good books should really end happily. I was trying to think of what the end should be. My Aunt Marno enjoyed entertaining and eating out and one of her favorite recipes was this very simple — but elegant — rum-raisin dessert. Coffee - Tea - Dessert. This can be served in Hyde Park or Westwood or somewhere in between. Have fun with this cookbook and do try this great dessert!

Keep cooking Cincinnati always — Cheri

RUM RAISIN DESSERT

1 pound cake: sliced
vanilla ice cream: sliced or scooped
rum raisins (soak raisins in dark rum – 12 hours)
chocolate sauce
*Optional: whipped cream

SERVE:
1 slice of cake
Topped with: vanilla ice cream
Topped with: rum raisins
Topped with: chocolate sauce and
*Optional: whipped cream

YOUR LOCAL RECIPE FINDS ~

FROM THE KITCHEN OF:

INGREDIENTS:

DIRECTIONS:

YOUR LOCAL RECIPE FINDS ~

FROM THE KITCHEN OF:

INGREDIENTS:

DIRECTIONS:

*I could not have done this book
without the following special people:*

Erin Beckloff: iNkY WiNKe
Erin is the wonderful graphic artist whose work made my
recipes and stories look even better. Thank You Erin!

Thanks to My Family especially, my Aunt Marno Christensen,
and Uncle Chris Christensen for their crazy lives and
collection of recipes from them and their friends.
Thanks to Emil and Bettyann Dickey.
Thanks to all the Swiss, Alsatians and Slovakians who ate
soup for generations!

Dear Friends – All of You!
My support network of fellow travelers who maintained
morale during this journey. Some of you include: Gayle
Stoddard, Linda Kovach, Catherine Estill, Sister Virginia
Dickey, MaryLou Berning, Millie Henley,Diana Whitener,
Kathleen Marcaccio, Judy Garshelis, Darlene Blasing,
Francesca Blasing, Moira and Mike Layman, Robert
Moreland, Jim Hodson, Thom Moon, John Blasing, Sandi
Cloppert, Mary Alice Wolf, Audrey Giles...and many many
others.

If your name isn't listed (due to space) it IS engraved
also upon my heart. Special people all!

ABOUT THE AUTHOR

Cheri Brinkman has lived much of
her life in Cincinnati and is an avid cook.

She has enjoyed numerous career "adventures"
including, fashion model, actress, singer as well as
working in the broadcasting field with her most
exciting adventure being a public speaker and writer.

Cheri is a graduate of Monterey Peninsula College
and the University of Cincinnati. In recent years
she has been a college educator with U.C.,
Miami and DeVry Universities teaching
communications classes.

cincinnatandsoup@yahoo.com